The Tutor's Handbook
READING
Grade 3

Written by Q. L. Pearce

Illustrated by Emilie Kong

Project Manager: Ellen Winkler
Editor: Christine Hood
Book Design: Rita Hudson
Cover Art Direction and Design: Rita Hudson and Riley Wilkinson
Cover Photos: Anthony Nex Photography
Graphic Artist: Carol Arriola

FS122122 The Tutor's Handbook: Reading Grade 3
All rights reserved—Printed in the U.S.A.
Copyright © 2001 Frank Schaffer Publications, Inc.
23740 Hawthorne Blvd., Torrance, CA 90505

TABLE OF CONTENTS

YOUR GOALS AS A READING TUTOR

ents, teachers, and in many cases, tutors. The goal of the tutor is to improve fluency and comprehension, and so improve school performance, while at the same time fostering a love of reading and books. As a tutor, you become a child's coach, guide, model, and confidence builder. In partnership with teachers and parents, you motivate the child to take an active role in the reading process and to view him- or herself as a capable reader.

This book will guide you in developing a plan of action for helping a child improve in reading. It also promotes the use of writing to help with reading comprehension. All of these abilities will help your student excel in school. This book will also provide you with tools for evaluating the child's progress and will offer suggestions on just what to say to a child, whether he or she is discouraged or encouraged. Are you ready? You can do it! Get your hand ready for some high fives, because the tutoring is about to begin!

Congratulations! You have made the decision to become a reading tutor. Tutoring a student can be challenging, fun, frustrating, inspiring, and can be all of those things for your student as well. It is sure to be a rewarding experience for both of you, as it is a special, one-on-one relationship in which both parties learn.

The love of reading is not something children are born with. The ability and desire to read are developed and patiently nurtured by caring par-

> **As a tutor, you become a child's coach, guide, model, and confidence builder.**

Get to Know Your Student

The first step in the tutoring process is to get to know your student. There are two reasons to form a comfortable bond with your student. The first is that the relationship between you and your student is unique. It's a one-on-one relationship where you work together very closely. You want your child to feel comfortable with you, comfortable enough to make mistakes, ask questions, be himself or herself. You also want your student to enjoy the sessions, look forward to them, have some laughs, and feel that learning can be fun. This can all be accomplished by the friendly way you interact. And as you get to know your student, with some of the material below to help, let your student get to know you, too, by sharing some of your own stories and interests. *Were you read to when you were young? What kinds of stories did you like? What made you gain a lifelong love of reading? In what ways has reading played an important role in your life?*

> **As you get to know your student, let your student get to know you, too, by sharing some of your own stories and interests.**

The second reason to get to know your student well is so that you can find reading material that will interest him or her. Books and other material that personally appeal to your student will give him or her an added reason to excel—because they can make reading great fun.

The following list contains some characteristics that third graders possess. Let this list help you understand the level and capabilities of your student, but don't hesitate to find some additional delightful qualities that are unique to your student.

What Are Third Graders Like?

- They are exuberant. Their enthusiasm propels them into learning with vitality.

- They are honest both in compliments and complaints. They express opinions without hesitation.

- They are imaginative. Give them a box of odds and ends and watch them create.

- They are determined. Involve them in a project or event and watch them go to work.

- They are friendly and seek many friendships with people of all ages.

- They are risk takers. They like to be the leaders and investigate new horizons.

- They are anxious to be the best they can be and need constant encouragement.

- They are discoverers. Problems become adventures to be conquered.

- They are ready to learn and grow with your direction and the ideas in this book.

Once the child is comfortable, explain that you would like to know more about him or her so that you can make the sessions more personal. Choose questions from the sample list that follows, or create your own. Enter his or her responses in your tutor's journal.

- Do you like to read at home?

- What is your favorite book?

- Does anyone read to you?

- Do you have brothers or sisters? If so, how old are they? Do they read?

- Tell me about your friends.

- Do you have pets?

- Do you have a hobby? What is it, and why do you enjoy it?

- What do you like to do for fun?

- What do you like best about school?

- What do you like least about school?

- What sports do you like?

- What do you like to read about?

- Do you read newspapers, comics, magazines?

- When you want to learn something, what do you do? (Ask? Read? Watch TV?)

- What would you like to learn more about?

- Do you like to draw?

- Would you like to be in a play?

- Do you like music?

- What do you like to write about?

- Do you ever write letters?

- Do you like surprises?

Children move toward independent reading more readily when they are given the opportunity to select their own reading material. Allowing a child to choose gives the student some control over a process that may at first seem foreign and even scary. It also makes reading more fun. You can make suggestions and try to steer a child toward different subjects, but if a child insists on reading the same books over and over, so be it! At least the child is reading—and loving it! You may get tired of the same stories time and time again, but you'll be amazed at how often a child can hear or read a favorite story without ever tiring of it.

Children are naturally curious about the world around them.

In your sessions with the child, tailor the books to his or her individual needs and general skill level, but offer a choice of topics. This way, a child will realize that he or she can read about a lot of different things. He or she can read a favorite folk tale and learn about dinosaurs, too! Children are naturally curious about the world around them. Show your student that reading both fiction and nonfiction can be fun and interesting. Fantasies and fairy tales are wonderful, but learning fun facts about insects, frogs, and firefighters can be equally fascinating. Once you know your student's interests, make a list of these topics on index cards. For example, if your student has a beloved dog, collects baseball cards, and likes bugs, label the cards *dogs, baseball,* and *insects.* Keep the cards available so you can jot down the names of books on each subject that may interest your student.

Does your student like writing, drama, or art? Does he or she enjoy chatting and answering your questions? There is a definite relationship between communication and reading skills. Take note and build on these strengths. Let your student act out a character's lines or draw a picture of a scene from a book. Does your student like surprises? If so, schedule surprise activities or vary the structure of the sessions accordingly to keep them interesting. If not, set up a basic structure and let the child know ahead of time if you plan to change it.

Story Starters

Would you like to gain some insight into what your student would enjoy reading? Story starters can help you find out which kinds of stories he or she enjoys. Read to the child one of the following story starters and ask him or her to complete the story and give it a title. Depending on his or her skill and comfort levels, have the child write or dictate the story for you. Before he or she begins, discuss the story starter and offer prompts such as the following:

Story Starter:

Peter sat at the edge of his bed. It was Saturday, but he had nothing to do. His best friend, Tim, was not at home. Tim had gone to visit his grandfather. Peter sighed and looked out the window. He wished he had a friend. Suddenly, he saw a flash of light as something zoomed into the backyard.

"What was that?" he said aloud. "I think I'll go and see."

Prompt:

What was in Peter's backyard?

Story Starter:

The village of Tarna was full of activity. On a hill high above, colorful flags topped the castle. Everyone was so excited at the news. A tiny new princess had been born during the night. The baker was baking a wonderful cake. The musician was hard at work on a special song. It seemed that everyone was busy, except Anna, the shepherd girl. She sat quietly in the barn, wiping tears from her eyes.

Prompt:

Why was Anna so sad?

Story Starter:

"Get up, sleepy head," Susan's dad said cheerily. "You have a soccer game this morning." Susan yawned and rolled out of bed.

"Okay, Dad," she answered. She pulled open her dresser drawer. "Where is my uniform?"

"I washed it last night," Dad replied. "Check the clothes dryer."

Susan ran to the kitchen. She popped open the dryer door and peered inside. Her jaw dropped open.

"Oh no!" she cried.

Prompt:

What did Susan see?

Your Student's Family

In some cases the struggling reader is a child whose parents have not fostered good reading habits in their home. Perhaps the parents never read aloud to their kids, or are illiterate. Or possibly there is not enough money for books, or the library is an unknown entity. Or it could be that the parents are too busy or too tired to read, or the television dominates the family's leisure time. As a tutor, you should be sensitive to the student and his or her family background.

Communicating with the child's parents or guardians will be an important factor in your success. To begin with, you will want to know what goals or concerns the parents have and how they compare to the child's. If you are planning on giving a child activities to do at home, make sure the parents have the time, materials, or skills needed to assist their child. Be aware of and sensitive to the differences among families. Try to find books that reflect your child's culture (as well as gender) and ones that include diverse cultures. Some cultures have a storytelling tradition as a way to share stories rather than writing them. Your student may be able to share some family stories with you. Some questions to consider:

- Does the family speak English as its primary language at home?

- Are there languages in addition to English that the child or family speaks?

- Can the parents read and write English?

- Do the parents and child have time available to work together on homework activities?

- Are there cultural differences that you need to be aware of that will affect how you and the child work together or how you and the parents work together? How does the family observe birthdays? Holidays?

As your tutoring sessions progress, be sure to communicate to parents what you are doing either through conversations or written notes or both. Here are some ideas you can suggest to the parents to encourage them to take a role in their child's reading progress:

- Show a personal interest in books and reading.

- Ask their child to talk about the books he or she reads.

- Invite their child to act out scenes from a favorite story.

- Read aloud to their child.

- Listen to their children read aloud.

- Visit the library together.

- Write encouraging notes to their child.

With a few adjustments, the same tutoring strategies included in this book can apply to English-language learners (ESL—English as a Second Language—students). If English is not read in the home, place particular emphasis on reading aloud. Different languages have different rhythms. Reading aloud will familiarize the child with the proper flow and inflection of English. Have the child sit beside you as you read so he or she can follow the text and see how written English compares to the spoken language.

The Importance of the Library

The library is a great resource for you and your student. Remember how cool it was to get your very first library card? Take your student to the neighborhood library and get him or her a library card. The child's parents will have to sign the application form because they will be the ones responsible for lost books. Some struggling readers have families that are not familiar with the library. If this is the case, consider yourself a tour guide, and invite the whole family on a field trip. Show the family the sections on books written in their language if English is not their first language, take them to the children's section and the adult section, and show them how to check out books. Knowing where and how to get books that are free of charge is a major step to becoming a life-long reader. And having Mom and Dad go to the library, too, provides great motivation for the young student.

A child who is learning to read needs a steady supply of books all the time. You can probably get some from the child's teacher, but don't depend on this. The teacher needs to be rotating the books he or she has throughout the classroom. Don't assume that you or the parents can buy all the books you will need; this would be too costly, and some books that you choose might end up being too easy or too hard. If they are from the library, you can just put them in the return slot if they aren't at the appropriate level. But if you bought them, then you'll feel committed to them. The librarian can direct you to books at the appropriate level for your student. You might want to explore the library's computerized catalog also. Your student can type in a favorite subject, such as *cats* or *bicycles,* and get a list of titles. There are also periodicals suitable for third graders at most libraries.

The following checklist provides additional ideas for helpful materials to have that encourage reading:

- restaurant menu
- telephone book
- encyclopedia
- map
- cookbook
- bus schedule
- comic book
- newspaper
- children's magazine
- song lyrics
- poetry
- word search and crossword puzzle
- word games such as *Boggle, Scrabble,* and *Concentration*

What You Need to Begin Tutoring

When in a tutoring session, you and your student must be comfortable. The setting you work in should help you both be comfortable and enable you to concentrate. You need a place that is quiet—with no television, no siblings interrupting you, and no friends knocking on the door wondering when you'll be finished so "Johnny" or "Jenny" can go out to play. Can you work in the local library? Perhaps you can find an empty classroom at the child's school, a quiet kitchen table, or maybe a corner of a living room. You will need a desk or table, a lamp or light bright enough to read comfortably by, paper, scissors, pencils, crayons, and a stapler. Wherever you are, be sure you can have this setting week after week, so that you and your student become assured of your place and committed to the routine of going there to learn. If you think that your student will not be too distracted by the surroundings, you can try working outdoors.

When moms and dads read to their children, it's usually a snuggly experience with lots of affection. When you read to your student, you cannot imitate that experience for a couple of reasons. One—it is not appropriate to become that physically close with your student. Two—you cannot replace the parents, even if you are committed to helping the child read. The experience will be different than that which the parents can give the child. It will still be valuable, however. You can sit shoulder to shoulder with the child; you can pat his or her hand or shake it. A good relationship with your student can be developed with some of the methods of praise listed below.

Ways to Encourage Your Student

Children need to receive positive feedback. They may not get individual attention in school, where they are one of dozens in a classroom. As a tutor, you can make your student feel valued for his or her efforts and accomplishments. Children thrive under these conditions. Think how great you feel when someone gives you a thumbs up for work you've done. Praise the behavior that you want to encourage. Here are some different ways to say "Good job!" to your student so that he or she will know that you really mean it.

Examples:

"Leslie, I noticed that you reread that phrase when you didn't understand it. That's what good readers do!"

"Ben, you have all of your supplies ready to use. Good for you! You are really well-prepared today."

"Maria, I'm enjoying reading aloud to you so much because you are listening very carefully. Thank you!"

By noticing improvement or positive effort, you are encouraging a child to strive to be even better the next time. The child will want to continue to do well. Sometimes, though, a child gets discouraged and requires finesse in handling. Learning to read is hard work, and the child may get tired and defeated at times. Be empathetic and encouraging to your student during these times. Realize that when you start to feel frustration, your student probably does, too, so you know just how he or she feels. Below are some methods for dealing with a frustrated student.

Examples:

"Reading is hard work, isn't it, Leslie? You're having trouble decoding this word. I'll bet you remember the strategy we used yesterday for the word *invisible*. Right! You remembered that we found a little word in the big word. What little word can you find in this word? Aha! That's very good."

"Ben, I know sometimes it's hard to think about what to write next in a story. Sometimes it just makes you want to throw your pencil out the window! I have an idea. Let's think of the craziest thing in the world that could happen next in your story. If it's a good idea, you can use it. If not, we'll think again." (By getting a child to laugh, you break down frustration levels. Ben may not use the crazy idea, but his creative juices will start flowing. Help him with another idea or two; then leave him to continue independently.)

"Maria, that sentence is a doozy! I can understand why you are having a bit of trouble with it. Let's break it down, word by word."

Rewards

Verbally praising a child for his or her good efforts as soon as you see a desired behavior is an effective way to encourage him or her to repeat the behavior. Praise from you is indeed a wonderful motivator. Sometimes, though, a child simply needs a treat—a sticker, a colorful pencil, an interesting eraser, a pad of sticky notes. These are things that third-grade girls and boys love. Also, remember your student's birthday. When it's your student's special day, stick a happy birthday sticker on his or her shirt, give him a birthday pencil or a little cupcake, and you will have a student who feels appreciated. The *Reading Award* reproducible, on page 63, can also be used to recognize your student's accomplishments.

Discipline

If a student is distracted, unfocused, or unwilling to work, you need to talk to him or her. Ask the child why he or she isn't trying. Listen to the response. The student may be tired, worried, hungry, nervous about problems at home, angry at a sibling—the list is endless. If the problem is serious, discuss it with the parents and teacher. Your student may be in a power struggle with you, as in "I'm not going to work and you can't make me." It's true—you can't really make a child work. At times like this it is important not to give up; you need to model perseverance and a commitment to your student. Let him or her know that you will still be there even when the student's behavior isn't perfect. If the student doesn't or can't concentrate on doing the work, then read aloud to him or her.

> **You need to model perseverance and a commitment to your student.**

You can try switching to another activity if your student is frustrated, unmotivated, or uncooperative. Switch to writing, have the child draw a picture of something you're reading together, or play with flash cards. Whatever you do, don't go away. Don't let the student win by making you angry or making you think helping him or her is hopeless. This child is at risk, and you, as a tutor, have great potential in recovering the child's reading ability. Stay put. You will win the child's respect, and he or she will be relieved to learn that this adult is not going to let him or her down.

Attitude

Some children have an I-can't-do-it attitude. Usually they can do it, but they want attention from you. First, you must decide if the work is at the proper level for your student's ability. Is the student genuinely attempting the task but looking dazed and confused? If so, the work is probably too difficult. Either help the child through it or give him or her something else to do.

The attention-seeking child will quickly glance at a task and give up before he or she tries. With this child, you need to be simple and direct: "I know you can do it. I'm going to set this timer and give you ten minutes to finish this job. Can you beat the clock? Go!" Urge this child to work independently. Then invite the student to say "I can do it!"

Children need to be reassured that they are capable of learning. Sometimes a task needs to be broken into smaller parts so that a child can successfully complete it. This strategy is important for developing a positive attitude. Children also need to know why learning is important. A struggling reader must realize that learning to read well will help him or her throughout life. How does a child realize this? Bring in your electric bill, a cereal box, insurance papers, a check book, a menu. Show the student all of the different kinds of things that adults must read. Talk about the consequences of not knowing how to read, such as not knowing what to order at a restaurant or having the electricity turned off because you didn't know where to send the check.

It's Okay to Make Mistakes

It *is* okay to make mistakes, and this is an important concept for a struggling reader. Teaching a child that it is okay to make a mistake gives him or her permission to take a risk. The student will feel free to try to blend a word or attempt to give an opinion about the meaning of a story. If the child makes a mistake, he or she will probably try again. If he or she looks at you for confirmation, you can simply say, "Think again" or "Does that make sense?" rather than, "No, you're wrong." Let the student know you trust him or her to discover the answer. Don't supply an answer after one wrong one from the student. Your job is to guide him or her down the correct road. If, after a while, the child doesn't get the answer, say "How about this?" and give it to him or her. Let the student affirm it. By assisting him or her in this reaffirming way, you will help the child develop a confident attitude.

Responsibility

One way a student is asked to be responsible is by completing homework assignments. A child who struggles in school could have poor homework habits. Successfully completing and returning homework develops responsibility in a child. It helps to tell a child that exercising makes our arms and legs and heart strong, and studying makes our brain strong. A tutoring session can be a time for a student to complete an assignment or have you go over the work with him or her. Many students have trouble remembering their assignments or materials needed to do the homework. As a coach, you can emphasize the following points to help a child establish good homework habits.

- **Structure** For example, do reading first, math second; finish one assignment before going on to the next. Work in an environment that is not distracting.

- **Organization** Does the student have all books, papers, supplies necessary and at hand? Does the student understand the assignment and have it in writing if necessary?

- **Routine** What is the best time each day for this particular child to do his homework? Does he or she need a snack before getting down to work?

Children work in different ways because people learn in different ways. Some children must have silence in order to work. Some must have the radio on in order to concentrate. Some students need short breaks between tasks. Some need to plow through without stopping until finished. What is important is to figure out what works for your student, and then to help him or her make this homework style a habit. If a child is having a problem with homework, figure out where the breakdown occurs. Remember, the teacher and the parents are there to support your efforts. Elicit their help in helping the child.

Helpful Hints

- Set simple, short-term goals. Small successes will increase your student's desire to reach a more difficult long-term goal.

- Set up a reward system or incentives for meeting short-term objectives.

- Make a check-off list of activities you hope to cover during the session. Give a star for each one completed.

- Don't overwhelm your student. If he or she is having a tough time, don't insist on completing the lesson plan.

- Don't pressure your student with comments such as, "You should be able to get this. It's easy," or "I told you the answer to this yesterday."

- Always praise effort, whether or not the child is doing things correctly. Give specific praise when applicable.

- Use a buddy system. Have your student read simple text to a younger child. This is beneficial for both children.

- End the session on a positive note. If the child has had problems with a book, finish up by having him or her read from a more familiar one.

- Your love of reading is contagious. Show it!

- Children are individuals. Learn what activities your student enjoys, what makes him or her laugh, and what topics interest him or her the most.

- Children learn best when they understand the goal. Involve your student in goal-setting.

- Variety is the spice of life! Provide a print-rich environment full of a myriad of fun and interesting, and easy as well as challenging, reading materials.

- Children learn from role models. Read aloud to your student and encourage his or her family to do so as well.

- Children also learn by doing. Have your student read aloud to you.

- There are multiple entry points into literacy. Incorporate writing, art, and drama into your sessions.

EVALUATING STUDENT READING LEVEL AND PROGRESS

Before you begin your first reading session, you will need to evaluate your student's reading skills. Speak to your student's teacher to find out which materials are used in class and how the child is doing with school work. When discussing the child's evaluation with the teacher, ask to see examples of his or her homework, tests, and report cards. The reproducible *Teacher Input Form,* on page 45, can help you when you meet with a teacher. Parents can also be helpful in assessment. Ask for their observations. *How does their child approach reading? What are his or her reading habits at home? Do they read to their child? Does their child feel comfortable around books and other text?*

Below are some general guidelines to look for when assessing a student's reading.

Does the reader . . .

- read for meaning, want to make sense of the text?

- read with fluency?

- use expression when reading aloud?

- understand punctuation, such as pausing at commas?

- reread?

- know when to skip a difficult word?

- sometimes pause to think about what's been read?

- use the illustrations to help understand the text?

- use reading strategies for difficult words or passages?

- enjoy reading?

If a student is not displaying the majority of these characteristics while reading third-grade level material, the student needs help achieving that level before going on to more difficult reading.

Assessing Student Progress

The areas you need to assess include *vocabulary, phonetic skills,* and *comprehension.* Assessment doesn't necessarily mean you must give a written test that results in a grade. You can assess a child's literacy skills while he or she is chatting, playing a game, or doing written activities.

Observe the child's book choices for free reading time. Ask why he or she made each choice. After the child has finished reading, ask him or her to rate the level of difficulty of the book. *Was it hard or easy?* Ask your student to evaluate his or her own performance. *How does the child feel about his or her reading? Where would he or she like to improve?* Invite the child to take notes on his or her own progress using a journal. Keep your own tutoring journal of notes from each session, including information such as books the child has read and progress made.

Vocabulary

There are direct links between vocabulary, comprehension, and fluency. To help you evaluate your student's vocabulary skills, use the *Word List* on page 46. Have your student read the words aloud while you note any that seem to pose a problem. *Is there a word pattern or family that causes the child to hesitate?* Have him or her circle any unfamiliar or particularly challenging words. Then use the *Vocabulary* worksheets on pages 46 through 51 to help you assess more of the child's vocabulary skills. Note any words that are used incorrectly.

Phonetic Skills

Words are composed of sounds, or *phonemes*. There are some 70 phonemes in the English language. Awareness of these sounds leads to the understanding of sound/symbol (letter) relationships, or *phonics*. A basic understanding of phonics enables a child to "sound out" unfamiliar words. To gauge your student's command of the basic phonemes, write out all the consonants in

> **Ask your student to evaluate his or her own performance.**

the alphabet. Ask the child to think of words that either begin or end with each letter. Point out that *C* and *G* have soft and hard sounds. If you prefer, offer the words yourself and have the child point out the letter and make the correct sound. Make note of any difficulties the child may have.

Use the *Phonetic Skills* worksheets on pages 52 through 56 to help you determine your student's command of the alphabet and the sounds the letters and blends make.

In addition to these activities, you can play a game of *I Spy* with your student. Look around the room and choose an object that your student must guess. Give a rhyming word as a clue. For example, "I spy with my little eye something that rhymes with *look*." The answer could be *book*.

If you determine that some phonics support is needed, begin sessions with activities that address the problem. Reciting short poems or jingles, singing songs, even playing with tongue twisters helps to develop *phonemic awareness* (recognition of sound/symbol relationships).

Comprehension

For reading material to have value and meaning, a child must understand the text. Students discover the overall meaning of what they read through clues such as *word order, sentence structure,* and *semantic cues* (meanings of individual words and phrases).

Learning the meanings of words and phrases and relating the printed word to that meaning is a complex process called *comprehension.* Use the *Comprehension* worksheets on pages 57 through 60 to help you evaluate your student's reading comprehension.

In addition to these activities, have your student read simple passages from several different books. Note how he or she deals with stumbling blocks to comprehension presented by such elements as homonyms (words that sound alike but have different meanings and spellings—*to, too, two*) and synonyms (words that have the same meaning). Watch for your student to use reading strategies when determining the meaning of a word or passage, such as:

• Making an educated guess

• Scanning the text or illustrations for clues

• Rereading

You may also have the child help you make word cards. Write 10 verbs on individual index cards. Do the same for nouns, adjectives, adverbs, and other parts of speech. When you are finished, invite your student to mix and match the cards to make up his or her own sentences.

Guide to Reading Levels

Once you have assessed your student's reading skills, you will be better able to select books to fit his or her needs. The following is a general guideline for matching skills to reading levels. A child often responds to a range of materials depending on his or her interests, so keep a variety of books on hand for each session.

> **The areas you need to assess include vocabulary, phonetic skills, and comprehension.**

Level 1
Student's Reading Skills:

- comfortable with phonemes
- comfortable with a vocabulary of core sight words
- reads familiar books with prompting
- needs full support with new material
- limited comprehension during independent reading

Select predictable books with simple vocabulary, repetitive text or rhyme, and illustrations on every page.

Level 2
Student's Reading Skills:

- reads simple, familiar books independently
- reads silently
- needs prompting with new material
- shows greater comprehension during independent reading

For a Level 2 reader, choose predictable books with controlled vocabulary and illustrations.

Level 3
Student's Reading Skills:

- increased vocabulary
- reads familiar books with confidence
- needs prompting with new material
- has confidence with rereading
- good comprehension during independent reading
- able to discuss text

Choose chapter books with a wider vocabulary and more complex storylines.

STRATEGIES FOR TEACHING READING

In a supportive learning environment, every child can learn to read. It is your job, as tutor, to equip the child with reading skills and strategies, support the child's efforts, and provide him or her with appropriate reading materials.

A "Rule of Thumb"

In most cases, what is suitable reading material depends on the child. When selecting books for your student, or evaluating a book that he or she has selected, use this general "rule of thumb": Open a book to any page, and ask the child to read it. As he or she begins, hold your hand where the child can't see it, fingers out. Every time your student comes to a word that he or she cannot read without your help, lower one finger. If you have to use your thumb (or fifth finger) before the student finishes the page, the book is too difficult. That doesn't mean it must be eliminated. If your student shows an interest in the book, don't discourage him or her. Use it when you apply such strategies as echo or partnered reading (see page 23). Keep in mind that you will need a wide range of books depending on whether you intend to use them for instruction, oral reading, or silent reading.

Favorite Books

Select some books that the child has already read and enjoyed. You can even offer stories that the child is familiar with from storytelling or movies. Consider well-known fairy tales, such as *Cinderella* or *Snow White,* that are told often or have appeared on film. Repetition is very helpful in reading. As *emergent readers* (those just beginning to learn to read), children often choose to read the same book over and over. It is comfortable and familiar. Familiarity enables a child to fill in the gap when he or she doesn't know a word, and rereading enhances comprehension. You can reinforce this strategy by offering several books on the same theme.

Selecting a New Book

When introducing a new book to a child, predictability is a plus. Predictable books that incorporate rhyme, repetition, common story structure, and/or predictable outcomes offer important clues to the reader. They help a child to successfully guess what makes sense in context or what works with the rhythm. Classic examples of such books

> **Books and other material that personally appeal to your student will give him or her an added reason to excel—because they can make reading great fun.**

are *Green Eggs and Ham* by Dr. Seuss (Random House, 1960) and *If You Give a Mouse a Cookie* by Laura Joffe Numeroff (Harper, 1994).

> **Children are individuals. Learn what activities your student enjoys, what makes him or her laugh, and what topics interest him or her the most.**

A picture is worth a thousand words. Illustrations can delight the reader, capture his or her attention, and guide him or her through the text. Illustrations that follow the text give important clues. When introducing your student to an illustrated book, allow him or her to scan the pictures and determine the storyline before reading.

Also remember that humor is a great learning tool as well as motivator. Joke books, riddles, silly stories, humorous poems, and even wacky tongue twisters can entice an otherwise reluctant reader.

Reviewing Books Ahead of Time

Before you offer a book to your student, read it through and note any pertinent information that he or she should have, such as new phrases, slang, foreign words, locations, or uses for objects that may be unfamiliar. Look for appropriate places to ask questions. Be prepared for your student to ask questions of you. Do not use prepared questions if they will interrupt the flow during the actual reading, but look for those "teachable moments," which can fall between chapters, before the next page, or when the child hesitates at certain words or ideas.

Choose picture books with rich or interesting illustrations that will give the two of you opportunities for interaction and discussion. Illustrations enhance a story as well as give clues to the content

of the material.

Previewing Books with Your Student

Preview new books with your student before you read. Allow him or her to spend an ample amount of time previewing the book with you:

- Read the title, look at the cover, and ask, "What do you think the book will be about?"

- Preview chapter headings or the table of contents, if there is one.

- In a nonfiction book, point out the glossary and index. Explain that they are there to aid the reader.

- Look at the illustrations together and take some time to talk about them.

- Read the flap or back cover copy and captions under photographs for more information.

- Discuss the author's or illustrator's other books, if the student knows of them.

- Encourage your student to make connections with his or her personal life.

• Ask the child to make predictions—think about what the book may be about, who the main character may be, what the character's problems or goals may be, and how the story may end. (Invite the child to use the reproducible *I Predict . . .* worksheet on page 62 to make predictions about the book.) The child can make predictions at the beginning of the story, before each new chapter, before the climax of the story, right before the end, and anywhere else you feel is an appropriate place to stop and reflect.

Using Background Knowledge

Children learn more readily if they can connect new information to something they already know. Give the child time to list or think about his or her background knowledge before beginning reading. For example, if the book is a fantasy tale about dragons, ask the child to think about what he or she already knows about a dragon's physical characteristics, behavior, and where one may be found. Making comparisons gives the child more background knowledge to build on. Ask your student to think about how the subject matter relates to his or her own life. For example, if you are reading a book about a snowman, you could ask questions such as:

• *Have you ever made a snowman?*

• *Do you like to play in the snow?*

• *What time of the year does it snow?*

• *What do you like to do in the winter?*

• *What are some of the things that happen in wintertime?*

Readers use background experience to bring meaning to a story. If the book is nonfiction, ask your student what he or she knows about the subject. Create three columns on a sheet of chart paper labeled *What I Know, What I Want to Learn, What I Learned*. In the first column, have the child write a few things he or she already knows about the subject, and in the second column, what he or she would like to learn. After reading, ask your student to add things he or she learned during reading to the third column so that progress can be seen.

What I Know	What I Want to Learn	What I Learned
Snow is cold.	What makes it snow?	
Snow is fun!	Are any two snowflakes alike?	
You have to wear warm clothes to play in the snow.	What is the difference between snow and sleet?	

Reading Poetry

The rhythm and rhyme of poetry help children become comfortable with language. Lighten the mood and prepare the child for the session by reading a short, entertaining poem that plays with or explores language. Have your student read along silently. When you are finished, read the poem together. Have the child close his or her eyes and describe any images the poem brings to mind. Then ask the child to draw pictures based on those images. *Jaha and Jamil Went Down the Hill: An African Mother Goose,* by Virginia Kroll (Charlesbridge, 1995), is a fun book of poems. It contains Mother Goose rhyme patterns with lyrics about African life.

Listening Skills

In general, many third graders are better listeners than readers. They can understand more complex stories than they can read, so you can choose more challenging books when you read aloud.

Students learn from modeling. Listening to you read gives the child a model to emulate when rereading a book. Engage the child's interest by employing dramatic tone and facial expressions during reading. Raise your eyebrows in surprise,

> **Listening to you read gives the child a model to emulate when rereading a book.**

increase your pace when a character is feeling anticipation or excitement, whisper, growl, or squeak–whatever it takes to make the words come alive!

As you read aloud, think aloud as well. Pause to ask yourself questions about meaning: *Why did the author use this word? Is it a clue? How does the main character feel about this new character?* Thinking aloud demonstrates a valuable strategy that becomes second nature as a reader progresses.

Being read to increases vocabulary and verbal expression. It gives a sense of how the rhythm and flow of fluent reading sounds. To help your student become a better listener, let him or her know what to listen for. Ask the child to pay special attention to pauses and emphasis. During your review, pick out some information for the child to listen for, such as: *What is the main character's favorite color?* or *How many people are in this character's family?* Ask questions about the context when you are finished to assess comprehension. Have the student retell the main points of the story. Together, imagine what may have happened next after the ending. To extend the experience, ask your student to draw a picture of one of the characters or design his or her own book cover.

If possible, provide an audio tape that the child can take home with a favorite book. He or she can listen to the tape while reading along. You can make the tape yourself, or ask the student to read aloud with you.

Oral Reading

Reading together orally, one-on-one, is one of the great strengths of the student/tutor relationship. It allows the student to follow a model while testing his or her own skills, to read a more challenging book, and to exchange ideas about the book. There are a variety of ways to approach oral reading.

Echo Reading

In *echo,* or *repeat reading,* read a line aloud, then have the student read it right after you. This gives him or her a chance to compare what a word looks and sounds like. This works particularly well with poetry because of the natural breaks in the text. Pause long enough for the child to comfortably read his or her part.

Have the student retell the main points of the story.

Partnered Reading

Echo reading can easily blend into *partnered reading.* For partnered reading, begin by reading slightly ahead of your student and having him or her read along silently. Gradually allow the child to take over and read aloud. If he or she is nervous, develop a hand signal that can be used when the child is comfortable and ready to continue on alone. Don't back off until you get the signal.

Check for Comprehension

When you have finished reading a book, check for comprehension by asking the child to point out a passage that described a part of the plot. You may also ask the child to point out the main challenge or problem, the climax of the story, how the problem was solved, and so on.

Another good way to check comprehension is to choose a new or difficult word from the text and write it down. Discuss how it was used and what it means. Ask the child why he or she thinks that particular word was chosen by the author. Have the child make up a sentence using the word. Invite the child to think of other words that have the same or similar meanings.

A comprehension check can also center around characters. Ask the child about his or her favorite character in the story and give reasons why. *Can the child relate to this character in some way?*

Rereading

Rereading aloud is a great confidence-builder. After reading a book with the tutor or alone, the child already has a set of expectations, plenty of clues, and a chance to test his or her skills. And it gives you the opportunity to observe your student's reading habits and fluency.

Do not stress word-for-word reading of the text if comprehension is evident. Accept a word substitution if it doesn't change the meaning. When the child stops at a word, give him or her a minute to figure out how to handle it. If you want to interact as the child reads, allow him or her to reach the end of the sentence before stopping for any reason—then keep interruptions brief. Make notes for longer exchanges after the story is finished. After a rereading, point out word meanings, punctuation, word repetition, and other interesting aspects of the text.

When help is needed during rereading, keep it general at first, coaching the student to try various

strategies. Suggest that the child:

- try to figure out a word by rereading the entire sentence.

- ask him- or herself, *Does that sound right?*

- ask him- or herself, *What word would make sense here?*

- use clues such as illustrations and photos.

- read ahead in a passage to get context clues, then reread the sentence with the difficult word.

- try blending the letters of the word aloud.

- sound out the beginning sound, the ending sound, the middle sound or the vowel sound, and then try to say the word.

- find smaller words within the word, then guess what the word is.

- break the word down into manageable groups of letters to sound out.

- ask for help when needed.

When the student is stuck on a word, you may decide to model "sounding out" the word, or simply say the word. If the word is not critical to general comprehension, you may have your student write it down on an index card so that you can look it up together later.

For example, consider this sentence: *The raft was made from balsa wood and reeds.* If your student has a problem with the word *balsa*, you could continue and discuss the word later. What the student *needs* to understand is that the raft is made of wood. In this case, the type of wood doesn't affect comprehension. The overall goal is to employ the scaffolding approach to corrections. This means to build on the child's previous knowledge. For example, you could ask the child what he or she thinks balsa might be, if he or she knows of any wood that begins with the letter *b*, if he or she has seen a raft before, etc.

Use the following suggestions as ways to support your student's attempt at self-correction.

- Praise your student's attempts at self-correction.

- As your student gains confidence in his or her reading strategies and skills, withdraw or delay verbal support during reading.

- Encourage your student to make more choices and take more responsibility.

- To assess your student's skill at oral reading, ask yourself:

  Does he or she read smoothly?

  Does he or she read in meaningful phrases?

  Does he or she read with expression appropriate to the text?

If the answers to the above questions are "yes," the child's reading would be considered fluent. If the child reads haltingly, the book may be too difficult.

When your student is comfortable with a book or passage, boost self-esteem by having him or her read to a younger child. This could be a younger sibling, or a student in a school or tutoring program. It is a fun and rewarding way to encourage fluency.

> **Encourage your student to make more choices and take more responsibility.**

Retelling

When you think your student has mastered a book, have him or her retell the story. Retelling a story from memory aids in comprehension. Ask your student to tell you the main characters and points from the book. Pay attention to event order and emphasis to determine where retelling is strongest.

A good way to assess if a child has understood the main events/ideas in a story is to make sure his or her retelling includes answers to the questions *who, what, when, where, why* and *how*. If your student can answer these questions, he or she has a good understanding of the story.

If necessary, begin with a guided retelling. Have your student respond to questions such as:

- *Where does the story take place?*

- *When does it take place?*

- *Who is the story about?*

- *Who else is in it?*

- *What is the main character's goal or problem?*

- *What happened?*

- *How did it end?*

Silent Reading

Silent reading may work well for some students at the beginning of a lesson. It offers time to rehearse and become familiar with a book before committing to it. For the most part, though, silent reading comes at or near the end of a session. Allow the child to reread a newly introduced book at his or her own pace, or revisit a familiar book.

Response Journal

One way to allow a child extended interaction with a book and create a personal relationship with it is by having him or her use a response journal. This is a simple notebook the child can use to reflect on his or her feelings about the story, characters, illustrations, or anything else the child wishes. Ask your student to write down any thoughts or feelings he or she has about the book. Sharing the journal will help you to assess comprehension. If the child is uncomfortable with writing, allow him or her to dictate journal entries for you to write down. The reproducible *My Book Review,* on page 61, can also be used to record the student's reactions to the reading material.

Ask your student to write down any thoughts or feelings he or she has about a book.

Using Prompts

Prompts are properly timed suggestions reminding the child to use strategies and clues when reading. When your student stops at a word, there are a number of things that you can do, such as:

- Suggest a clue in the illustration. *What is the girl in the picture holding?*

- Link the word to the child's background knowledge. *You like to play baseball. What position do you like to play?*

- Link the word to recent reading. *The boy in yesterday's story got one for his birthday.*

- Use a visual prompt. (Sometimes a motion or hand signal is enough.)

- Suggest using an educated guess. *Try rereading this sentence. What word makes sense here?*

- Read ahead to look for clues. *What sound does the word begin with? Can you think of a word with that sound that would fit in this sentence?*

- Suggest alternatives. *Let's skip the word for now. Maybe as we read on, we'll find other clues that can help us figure it out.*

If the word is important to the meaning of the sentence, and your student cannot figure out what it is, you can tell him or her the word. Allowing too much time will disrupt comprehension. Whether you supply the word or the child figures it out, have him or her reread the sentence.

Praise the child's effort, whether it was successful or not. This is extremely important to a child's self-confidence. Your student needs to understand that trying and failing, as well as success, are all part of the learning process.

More Strategies

There are several additional techniques you can use for guiding a developing reader. Try some of the following strategies to enhance your student's reading skills.

Games and Puzzles

Word games such as *Bingo*, riddles, and puzzles are all fun and entertaining ways to make a child comfortable with language. Word songs and chants such as jump rope rhymes and Mother Goose verses are also fun ways to learn. Try some of the methods that follow when your student needs a break from reading.

Cloze Passages

Cloze passages are chunks of text with words missing. The child is then asked to fill in appropri-

> **Trying and failing, as well as success, are all part of the learning process.**

ate words, or those that make sense, to complete the passage. Cloze passages help the child learn to search for clues in context. To create a cloze passage, make a copy of a page from a book with which your student is familiar. White out several key words and then make a clean copy. Ask your student to read the text and fill in the missing words. Begin the exercise with predictable text or poems. Once your student can handle the exercise with confidence, select a more challenging passage.

Rebus Stories

Rebus stories replace words with pictures. These stories are a fun way to encourage the reader to use clues to decide which word fits best in a sentence. Books of rebus stories are available in bookstores, some grocery stores, and teacher supply stores. You can even make your own rebus stories using a copy of a page of text. You'll need a poem or familiar story with repetitive text and some small stickers or rubber stamps. Photocopy the page. Then choose a single word that is repeated several times and cover it with a sticker or stamp. Have your student read the text and fill in the missing word.

Dictated Reading

Dictated reading allows a child to connect written and spoken language. After your student has finished reading familiar text, ask him or her to retell the story as completely as possible. Write down what he or she says without editing. Have the child read the dictated sentences aloud to you.

Elkonkin Boxes

Elkonkin boxes are useful in developing phonemic awareness. Choose a few words, such as *shine, love,* and *baby*. With your student, enclose each of the phonemes, or independent sounds, in Elkonkin boxes, as shown in the examples below. When your student understands the concept, choose several words from a passage of text and guide him or her in singling out each phoneme.

sh	i	ne

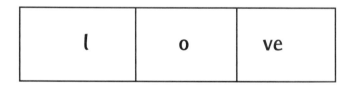

l	o	ve

b	a	b	y

THE TUTORING SESSION

Prompt the reader to use strategies and clues when reading.

A tutoring session can last anywhere from 15 minutes to an hour. The following is an example of how a tutor (we'll call her "Mrs. Gonzales") might conduct an hour-long session. This is only a *suggested plan*, since the needs of no two children are exactly alike, nor will children respond to tutoring in an identical manner. Mrs. Gonzales's student (we'll call him "Jeff") is a third grader.

The session is divided into four parts. They are summarized here and then described at more length on the pages that follow.

Warm-up (10 minutes): The warm-up is designed to put the student at ease, bolster his self-image as a reader, and prepare him to work. During this time, Mrs. Gonzales reads aloud and then asks Jeff to read aloud.

Focused reading (25 minutes): The bulk of the session is devoted to this activity. New material is introduced, there is opportunity for assessment, and problems can be addressed.

Five-minute break.

Relaxed reading (15 minutes): The student spends 10 minutes of this time in silent reading and five minutes doing an activity of his choice.

Wrap-up (5 minutes): Student and tutor use the last five minutes to wrap up, discuss the session, and make plans for the next session.

Warm-up

Jeff responds well to humor, so Mrs. Gonzales has chosen the following silly poem to read as a warm-up.

Tommy Allen Tuttle
came home at half past three
to find a great blue snivel
snagged in his tall peach tree.

No one seemed to notice
that the feathered thing was near,
although it sobbed quite loudly
and cried inky snivel tears.

Tommy made a plan.
He knew what he would do
to save the tree-bound snivel,
which was six feet tall and blue.

He sawed right through the branch
and set the snivel free,
but its tears had stained the blossoms
that sprouted from the tree.

Now the tree bears dark blue peaches,
and only Tom knows why.
He smiles about his secret
as he eats his bluepeach pie.

Mrs. Gonzales reads the poem aloud in a pleasant, rhythmic manner. She then asks a few questions to support Jeff's understanding of the characters in the poem.

Mrs. Gonzales: What do you think a "snivel" is?

Jeff: Some kind of bird or something.

Mrs. Gonzales: Can you describe it to me?

Jeff: It's really big with blue feathers. And it can fly.

Mrs. Gonzales: Do you think there really is such a thing?

Jeff: No. I think it's just made up.

Mrs. Gonzales: What kind of boy is Tommy?

Jeff: He's nice, I guess. He helped the bird.

Mrs. Gonzales: Do you think Tommy just imagined the snivel?

Jeff: No, because the peaches turned blue. That means it was really real, just nobody else could see it or hear it.

Mrs. Gonzales: Good. I like the way you explained that. I'll read it one more time. Why don't you read along with me silently?

Jeff: Okay.

> **The rhythm and rhyme of poetry help children become comfortable with language.**

After reading the poem, Jeff is ready to read a familiar book alone. Mrs. Gonzales gives him a selection of books that he has read before. He likes building things, so he chooses a nonfiction picture book about bridges. It is the third time he has read this book. Mrs. Gonzales asks him to read the first few pages aloud. As he reads, she listens for fluidity and emphasis. Jeff pauses uncertainly at a word, and she waits as he rereads the sentence and looks at the photograph on the page. He does not look at her or ask for help, so she does not prompt him. She can hear him sounding out the first letters under his breath, and then he says the word and continues on. She can tell that he is using a variety of reading strategies, and she jots this down in her journal.

Focused Reading

Mrs. Gonzales has reviewed a chapter book called *Where's Willie?* by Todd Parker. It is illustrated with simple black-and-white line drawings. She feels that it might pose a slight challenge, but since the main character is Jeff's age and Jeff loves dogs, it will engage his interest. She shows him the cover.

Mrs. Gonzales: I thought you might like this story. Can you see why?

Jeff: It has a scottie dog in it.

Mrs. Gonzales: That's the kind of dog you have, isn't it?

Jeff: Yes. His name is Blitzen.

Mrs. Gonzales: This dog's name is Willie. It's in the title of the book. Can you tell me anything about the book from the title?

Jeff: *Where's Willy?* I think the dog hides . . . no, I think he gets lost.

Mrs. Gonzales: Let's look at the chapter headings. Maybe we can find out more.

Together, they review the chapter headings and some of the illustrations. Jeff says that the boy's name is Kyle. He and his parents are spending the summer at the beach. Jeff predicts that Willie gets lost. Kyle and his parents look for him. Willie makes friends with several different people.

Mrs. Gonzales: How do you suppose the story ends?

Jeff: I think they find him.

Mrs. Gonzales: What would you do if your dog got lost?

Jeff: I'd ask lots of people, and I'd put up posters with his picture and stuff.

Mrs. Gonzales: Let's see what Kyle does.

Jeff (reading): "'Time to get up,' Kyle's mom c . . . call." *(pause)* "'Time to get up,' Kyle's mom called. Kyle sat up and . . ." *(Jeff pauses, looks at the text and then looks at tutor)*

Mrs. Gonzales: Will this illustration help?

Jeff: He's yawning. *(reading)* "Kyle sat up and yawned."

Mrs. Gonzales: Good. I like the way you used the picture as a clue. That's a good reading strategy.

Mrs. Gonzales does not prompt Jeff when he reads the word *called* incorrectly. She gives him time to self-correct. When he does, she notes it in

> **Give the reader time to use reading strategies. When a reader is able to figure out a word without being told, this boosts self-confidence.**

her journal. She gives him time to use his reading strategies when he reaches the word *yawned*. When he looks to her for help, she directs him to a clue in the illustration so that he is able to figure out the word without being told. This boosts his self-confidence. Mrs. Gonzales also draws attention to his success by offering specific praise.

Jeff continues to read for three pages with several more prompts. When he has finished, Mrs. Gonzales asks him to summarize what he has read in a retelling. After he retells the story, she asks some questions to further check his comprehension.

Mrs. Gonzales: Was Kyle happy that they were going to stay at the beach for the summer?

Jeff: Yes.

Mrs. Gonzales: Was he worried about anything?

Jeff: He didn't know if he would find any friends.

Mrs. Gonzales: What was something he liked to do at the beach?

Jeff: He liked to make sand castles.

Mrs. Gonzales: Have you ever made a sand castle?

Jeff: No. When I'm at the beach, I stay in the water the whole time.

Mrs. Gonzales: I think Kyle likes to swim, too. And so does Willie. See—the next chapter is called "Splashing Around." Why don't you write what you know about the story in your journal, and then we can stop for a cold drink.

In his journal, Jeff writes that Kyle is going to the beach. His dog is going, too. They like playing in the sand. While Jeff writes, Mrs. Gonzales makes notes in her own journal.

Relaxed Reading

After the break, Mrs. Gonzales has Jeff read silently for 10 minutes. He chooses to reread the beginning of the story again and then look at the rest of the illustrations. This makes him feel comfortable with the text he will be reading at the next session.

Wrap-up

In the few minutes left at the end of the session, while Jeff waits for his ride home, he and Mrs. Gonzales play a game. They take turns coming up with a list of all of the things that can be found during a day at the beach.

Additional Activities

The following activities can be used to fill in those few extra minutes when the session is over and encourage a young reader in a variety of ways.

> **Help the child realize how important print is in his or her daily living.**

Dear Author

If your student has read and enjoyed a recently published book, help him or her write to the author in care of the publisher's address. Suggest that he or she ask questions, such as:

- *How did you get started?*
- *How do you get your ideas?*
- *What is your favorite book?*

Words All Around

To show your student that reading is a meaningful and important part of everyday life, walk around your tutoring area together and list all the places that the printed word is found. Don't overlook such things as the printing on a light switch, the labels in your clothing, and the money in your wallet. Ask the child to make a similar list at home and bring it to the next session. Study both lists, and then ask your student to make up a story about a day in the life of a child who lives in a land with no reading or writing. This will encourage the child to realize how important print is in his or her daily living.

To extend on this idea, ask your student to list ways he or she uses print or sees print being used during a one-week period. Ideas may include:

- stop sign
- school name on building
- street sign
- recipe
- label on medicine bottle
- newspaper/magazine
- instructions for a puzzle
- flyer for a lost pet
- keyboard
- calendar

What's That Number?

Open the telephone book to the yellow pages. Ask your student find a variety of listings, such as a store that sells tropical pets, an Italian restaurant, and a dentist.

Clipping Compounds

This activity is great for spelling and vocabulary practice. Ahead of time, hang up a simple rope or clothesline. Then use a black marker to write words that could be parts of compound words on the flat side of clothespins. Some examples include:

any/one	bee/hive	every/where	her/self
base/ball	star/fish	news/paper	your/self
birth/day	ear/ring	day/dream	scare/crow
tooth/pick	may/be	cow/boy	foot/print
mountain/top	snow/ball	milk/shake	sun/burn
earth/quake	eye/brow	work/shop	in/side
bag/pipe	class/mate	drive/way	some/one
button/hole	bird/house	butter/fly	sun/shine
sand/box	stage/coach	bed/room	door/knob

Ask your student to match clothespin pairs to make several compound words. Have him or her write each compound word on a strip of paper and clip it to the clothesline with the matching clothespins. Encourage your student to fill the entire clothesline!

Information, Please!

Bring in a selection of food cans and packages. Ask your student to find certain things on the label, such as:

• product name

• number of servings

• company name

• two ingredients

• expiration or freshness date

• cooking instructions

• fat or protein content

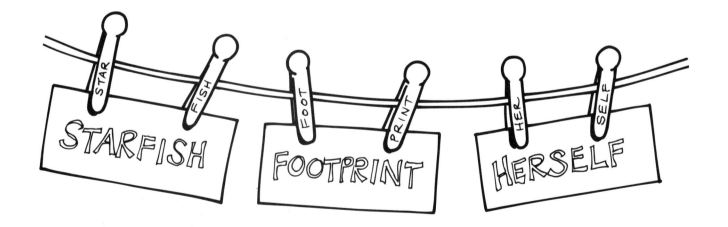

Remember that humor is a great learning tool as well as motivator.

"Reading" Television

Does your student like to watch television? The answer to this question will most likely be "yes." To help use television as a learning tool, ask your student to describe his or her favorite show. Just for fun, have him or her keep a pencil and paper on hand when watching this show. Tell the child to note every time a printed word is shown or referred to during the time the show is on. Ask the child to include commercials as well.

The child can also use this activity on a trip to the movies. Items on this list could include: movie posters, tickets, and concession stand goodies.

Guided Tour

Bring in a *TV Guide* or the schedule that appears in the daily newspaper. With your student, look through the schedule to find different items, such as:

- a sports show
- a comedy show
- an advertisement
- a children's show
- a cable movie
- a movie promotion
- a talk show

On the Road

Obtain a local map and bus schedule. With your student, plan several different trips, such as a shopping trip, a visit to the library or local bookstore, or a trip to an art museum and lunch at a favorite restaurant. Use the map and bus schedule to decide when and how you can get to your desired destinations. Invite your student to help you write down directions on how to get there, whether by bus or by car, as well as the estimated times of arrival.

RECOMMENDED READING

Bjork, Christina. *Linnea in Monet's Garden.* Lectorum Publications, 1996.
Take a trip to visit Monet's home near Paris. Beautifully illustrated by Lena Anderson. (picture book)

Brown, Marc. *Arthur Writes a Story.* Little Brown, 1998.
When writing a story, Arthur gets advice from many sources. Perhaps he gets too much advice. Additional titles in the series. (early reader)

Bunting, Eve. *Fly Away Home.* Clarion Books, 1993.
A boy and his father hope to have a home someday. Until then, they have to live in an airport terminal. (picture book)

Bunting, Eve. *The Wednesday Surprise.* Clarion Books, 1990.
As a surprise for her dad's birthday, Anna helps her grandmother learn to read. A touching and encouraging story. (picture book)

Burleigh, Robert. *Flight: The Journey of Charles Lindbergh.* Paper Star, 1997.
A wonderfully told biography of Charles Lindbergh. This account of the trans-Atlantic flight is inspiring. (picture book)

Books

Banks, Lynne Reid. *Houdini: The Amazing Story of an Escape-Artist Hamster.* Camelot, 1991.
The tale of a remarkable hamster rightfully named after the famous magician. In his own words, Houdini is "no ordinary animal." (chapter book)

Benjamin, Anne. *Young Harriet Tubman: Freedom Fighter.* Troll, 1992.
The biography of a brave woman fighting slavery in America. (early reader)

Clements, Andrew. *Double Trouble in Walla Walla.* Millbrook Press, 1997.
Lulu is having trouble speaking, and the whole school seems to be following along. This clever story is filled with clever word play. (picture book)

Cohen, Caron Lee. *The Mud Pony.* Scholastic, 1989.
A Pawnee folk tale of a boy and a pony made of mud. The pony comes to life and helps the boy find his own inner strength. (picture book)

Cole, Joanna. *The Magic School Bus Inside the Earth.* Scholastic, 1989.
Miss Frizzle takes her class for a special field trip deep into the earth to learn about rocks and minerals, and how the earth formed. Additional titles in the series. (picture book)

Danziger, Paula. *Amber Brown Goes Fourth.* Little Apple, 1999.
Amber Brown is entering the fourth grade. She confronts a wealth of problems, including the divorce of her parents, the moving away of her best friend, and the loss of the playground burping contest. Additional books in the series. (chapter book)

Danziger, Paula. *The Cat Ate My Gymsuit.* Paper Star, 1998.
Marcy Lewis doesn't have any friends, until she helps her favorite teacher. A humorous look at the problems of growing up. (chapter book)

De Paola, Tomie. *The Legend of the Poinsettia.* Paper Star, 1997.
A Mexican folk tale about the beautiful floral symbol of Christmas. (picture book)

Domanska, Janina. *The Turnip.* Macmillan, 1969.
Grandmother and Grandfather's turnip grows bigger and bigger every day. With much help, they are finally able to pull it out of the ground. (picture book)

Garza, Carmen Lomas. *Family Pictures/Cuaderos de familia.* Children's Book Press, 1993.
A young girl shares stories of family life in a traditional Mexican community in Texas. Text is in both English and Spanish. (picture book)

Gauch, Patricia Lee. *Thunder at Gettysburg.* Young Yearling, 1990.
A young girl finds herself in the middle of the battle of Gettysburg. While helping wounded soldiers, she learns that war is a terrible thing. (chapter book)

Goble, Paul. *Her Seven Brothers.* Bradbury, 1988.
A Plains Indian legend tells an intriguing story of a young girl's devotion to her seven brothers and the creation of the Big Dipper. (picture book)

Howe, Deborah and James. *Bunnicula.* Simon & Schuster, 1979.
A mysterious bunny is adopted by an unsuspecting family. The family cat is convinced the newcomer is a vampire, and his plans to expose the creature go hilariously awry. (chapter book)

Hurwitz, Johanna. *Aldo Applesauce.* William Morrow, 1979.
Aldo Sossi humorously faces the challenges and struggles of being the new kid in school. (chapter book)

Hutchins, Pat. *The Doorbell Rang.* Mulberry Books, 1989.
Two children are anxious to gobble down some yummy cookies! But they must share their treat when more children arrive. Includes lots of easy, fun repetition. (picture book)

Jones, John R. *Dinosaur Hunters.* Random House, 1989.
An overall view of paleontology, which includes general information about certain dinosaurs. (early reader)

Key, Alexander. *The Forgotten Door.* Scholastic, 1989.
A great book for fans of science fiction, this story tells of an extraterrestrial boy trying to find his way home. (chapter book)

King-Smith, Dick. *A Mouse Called Wolf.* Crown, 1997.
A tale of a talented and loveable young mouse told by the author of *Babe, the Gallant Pig.* (early reader)

Kinsey-Warnock, Natalie, and Helen Kinsey. *The Bear That Heard Crying.* Puffin, 1997.
A true story about a young girl who got lost in the woods and was protected by a bear. (picture book)

Krull, Kathleen. *Alex Fitzgerald's Cure for Nightmares.* Troll, 1998.
When nine-year-old Alex moves to California, she starts having nightmares. Good reader identification possibilities. (early reader)

Krull, Kathleen. *Maria Molina and the Days of the Dead.* Simon & Schuster, 1994.
Maria celebrates this Mexican holiday with her family. (picture book)

Krull, Kathleen. *Wilma Unlimited: How Wilma Rudolph Became the World's Fastest Woman.* Voyager Picture Book, 2000.
Wilma Rudolph needed a leg brace as a child. She went on to win three Olympic gold medals in track and field events. Krull gives the reader an inspirational view of this heroic woman. (picture book with photographs)

Lansky, Bruce, ed. *Girls to the Rescue: Tales of Clever, Courageous Girls from Around the World.* Meadowbrook Press, 1999.
A collection of interesting and inspiring stories about powerful girls. There are four more books in this series. (chapter book)

Le Guin, Ursula. *Catwings.* Orchard Books, 1999.
This book is a lovely introduction to the fantasy genre. It tells of the adventures of several small, winged kittens. (early reader)

MacLachlan, Patricia. *Sara, Plain and Tall.* HarperTrophy, 1987.
Anna and Caleb's mother has passed away. Papa chooses a new bride, and they must all learn how to be a family. (chapter book)

Mahy, Margaret. *The Great White Man-Eating Shark: A Cautionary Tale.* Puffin, 1996.
Norvin uses the fact that he looks like a shark to scare swimmers away from his favorite cove. In a laugh-out-loud twist, a real shark is fooled as well. (picture book)

Mahy, Margaret. *The Horribly Haunted School.* Viking, 1998.
This ghost story is full of plenty of laughs and a main character who is allergic to ghosts. (chapter book)

Martin, Rafe. *The Rough-Face Girl.* Paper Star, 1998.
An Algonquin version of Cinderella. (picture book)

Meddaugh, Susan. *Martha Walks the Dog.* Walter Lorraine, 1998.
The story of an amazing speaking dog who learns that a little praise goes a long way. Also see another book in the series, *Martha Speaks.* (picture book)

Naylor, Phyllis Reynolds. *Shiloh.* Macmillan, 1991.
A young boy befriends an abused dog, Shiloh, and lies to protect him from harm. (chapter book)

Osborne, Mary Pope. *Tonight on the Titanic.* Random House, 1999.
Their magic tree house takes Jack and Annie to the doomed ship. They must help two children find their way to a lifeboat. There are additional books in the Magic Treehouse series. (early reader)

Paek, Min. *Aekyung's Dream.* Children's Book Press, 1988.
Aekyung must adjust to a new life in a new land. Her heritage gives her the strength to adjust. The tale is told in Korean and English. (picture book)

Parish, Peggy. *Amelia Bedelia Goes Camping.* William Morrow & Co., 1997.
Amelia takes instruction literally, which leads to a series of crazy mistakes when her family goes camping. There are additional titles in the series. (early reader)

Park, Barbara. *Junie B. Jones Smells Something Fishy.* Random House, 1998.
Junie wants to take a pet to school for pet day, but dogs and cats are not allowed. She must find an interesting pet that won't cause too much trouble. There are additional books in the series. (early reader)

Pilkey, Dav. *The Adventures of Captain Underpants.* Scholastic, 1997.
Two kids hypnotize their principal into thinking he is the great Captain Underpants. Hilarious third-grade humor. There are more titles in the series. (chapter book)

Pilkey, Dav. *Dog Breath! The Horrible Terrible Trouble with Hally Tosis.* Scholastic, 1994.
The Tosis family dog, Hally, has a problem with bad breath. The family can't seem to find a way to solve it, but Hally finds it useful. (picture book)

Pinkwater, Daniel. *Author's Day.* Aladdin, 1997.
An author's visit to a school goes awry when Branwell Wink-Porter is praised for writing *The Fuzzy Bunny*—a book he didn't write. (picture book)

Pinkwater, Daniel. *Fat Men from Space.* Yearling Books, 1980.
Oh no! Men from space are stealing all of Earth's junk food! William, a young Earth boy, is picking up their transmissions in his tooth filling. (early reader)

Prelutsky, Jack. *Something Big Has Been Here.* William Morrow & Co., 1990.
A variety of poems that have humor in common. Young readers will giggle their way through the word play. (poetry)

Prelutsky, Jack. *A Pizza the Size of the Sun: Poems.* Greenwillow, 1996.
A great collection of short poetry. Plenty of word play and humor. Excellent read-aloud possibilities. (poetry)

Robinson, Barbara. *The Best Christmas Pageant Ever.* Harper Junior Books, 1972.
The disruptive Herdman kids cause apprehension when they become involved in the community Christmas pageant. (chapter book)

Rockwell, Thomas. *How to Eat Fried Worms.* Franklin Watts, 1973.
Billy bets he can eat 15 worms. A great storyline for reluctant readers. (early reader)

Rylant, Cynthia. *Henry and Mudge and the Bedtime Thumps.* Aladdin Paperbacks, 1996.
Henry is concerned about how his grandmother will take to his dog, Mudge. There are additional titles in the series. (early reader)

Sachar, Louis. *Wayside School Is Falling Down.* Avon, 1998.
The kids at Wayside School are always up to something. In this book, Toss gets a magic dog. There are additional books in the series. (chapter book)

Schwartz, Alvin. *Busy Buzzing Bumblebees and Other Tongue Twisters.* HarperCollins, 1992.
A delightful collection of tongue twisters children will love! (early reader)

Scieszka, Jon. *The Stinky Cheese Man and Other Fairly Stupid Tales.* Viking, 1993.
This collection of silly fairy stories keeps children laughing and reading. (picture book)

Scieszka, Jon. *The True Story of the Three Little Pigs.* Puffin, 1996.
The classic story retold from the wolf's point of view. (picture book)

Sharmat, Marjorie W. *I'm Terrific.* Holiday, 1977.
A young bear struggles to find a balance between arrogance and apathy, while learning valuable lessons in how to be a good friend. (picture book)

Sharmat, Marjorie Wienman. *Nate the Great and the Fishy Prize.* Young Yearling, 1988.
A young boy detective enters his dog in a pet contest, but the prize disappears. There are additional titles in the series. (early reader)

Silverstein, Shel. *Falling Up.* HarperCollins, 1996.
A collection of zany poems from Shel Silverstein. (poetry)

Silverstein, Shel. *Where the Sidewalk Ends.* HarperCollins, 1987.
Remarkable poems from silly to sad. (poetry)

Singer, Marilyn. *It's Hard to Read a Map with a Beagle on Your Lap.* Owlet, 1997.
Fun, catchy poems about dogs with mixed media illustrations. Very appealing for dog-loving kids. (poetry)

Sinykin, Sheri Cooper. *The Secret of the Attic*. Magic Attic Press, 1995.
Four girls become friends with a neighbor who allows them to explore her magic attic. They are transported on wonderful adventures. There are more books in the series. (chapter book)

Smith, Robert Kimmel. *Chocolate Fever*. Putnam, 1989.
Henry Green has the first recorded case of chocolate fever, which is the result of his love of the sweet treat. (early reader)

Soto, Gary. *The Cat's Meow*. Scholastic, 1995.
Graciela is amazed when her cat begins to speak in Spanish! (chapter book)

Steig, William. *Brave Irene*. Farrar, Straus & Giroux, 1988.
A young girl must brave a snowstorm to help her mother keep a promise. (picture book)

Van Leeuwen, Jean. *Amanda Pig, Schoolgirl*. Puffin, 1999.
Amanda has been waiting her whole life to go to school. Finally the day arrives, and she encounters new joys and challenges. There are additional books in the series. (early reader)

Waters, Kate. *Sara Morton's Day*. Scholastic, 1989.
A day in the life of a young girl living in the early American colony at Plymouth. Includes interesting photographs. (photo essay)

Weber, Bernard. *Ira Says Goodbye*. Houghton, 1988.
Ira must cope with a variety of emotions when he says goodbye to his friend Reggie, who is moving away. (picture book)

Wilder, Laura Ingalls. *Little House in the Big Woods*. Harper Junior Books, 1953, 1986.
The first in a series of nine books that detail the life experiences of a girl and her pioneer family. (chapter book)

Wisniewski, David. *Golem*. Clarion Books, 1996.
Wisniewski's cut-paper illustrations are captivating. This 400-year-old Jewish tale is full of magic and monsters. (picture book)

Zolotow, Charlotte. *The Quarreling Book*. Harper Junior Books, 1965.
A family spends a rainy day arguing, but the quarreling stops when father comes home in a happy mood. (picture book)

On the Net

Be aware that web-site addresses change frequently.

ALA (American Library Association) Parent's Page: A terrific listing of 700 sites for children preschool to age 14. It includes author sites, kids' writing, classics, reference materials, and publisher sites.
http://www.ala.org/parentspage/greatsites/

Dictionaries for every need, from foreign languages to specialized references:
http://www.facstaff.bucknell.edu/rbeard/diction.html

Random House Kids: Learn about the characters and books associated with Random House publishing. Also includes book reviews.
http://www.randomhouse.com/kids

Reading Rainbow: Find out more about the show and featured books.
http://gpn.unl.edu/rainbow/

KidNews: Kids writing about events and other kids. Also includes book reviews.
http://www.kidnews.com/

KidPub: 10,000 stories and poems written by kids from all across the globe.
http://www.kidpub.org/kidpub/

Scriptito's Place: For young writers' ages 7 to 15. Also includes story starters and contests.
http://members.aol.com/vangarnews/scriptito.html

KidsConnect: A question-answering service for grades K to 12. School library media specialists provide assistance.
http://www.ala.org/ICONN/kidsconn.html

Linkopedia Kid Zone: Web sites and activities that range from learning the ABC's to homework help.
http://www.linkopedia.com/kids.html

Series Sites:
Games, Activities, and Information on Books, Characters, and Authors

Baby-Sitters Club:
www.scholastic.com/annmartin/bsc/index.htm

Dr. Seuss's Seussville:
www.randomhouse.com/seussville/

My Little House on the Prairie Home Page:
www.com/~jenslegg/index.htm

Scholastic's Magic School Bus Fun Place:
www.scholastic.com/magicschoolbus/

Goosebumps:
www.place.scholastic.com/goosebumps/index.htm

Scholastic Animorphs:
www.scholastic.com/animorphs/

Arthur: The World's Most Famous Aardvark:
www.pbs.org/wgbh/arthur/

Berenstain Bears:
www.berenstainbears.com

Teacher Input Form

Name of child _____ Date _____

1 What is this child's reading level?

Nonreader   Pre-primer   Primer   First Grade   Second Grade   Third Grade

2 Rate the student's ability in the following areas:

(Use this key, comments, or both to record answers:

E = Excellent   VG = Very Good   G = Good   N = Needs Help)

a. Oral reading _____

b. Comprehension _____

c. Phonics _____

   beginning consonants _____

   short vowels _____

   long vowels _____

   consonant blends _____

d. Spelling _____

e. Writing _____

   Writing a story _____

   Capitalization and punctuation _____

   Handwriting ability _____

f. Speaking skills _____

g. Listening skills _____

h. Work habits _____

3 Is there any other information about this child you think would be helpful to know?

_____

_____

4 What do you think would be the best areas for me to focus on?

_____

_____

5 Do you have any materials you could share with me in those areas?

6 Could I have a copy of the writing paper and handwriting style you use in class?

Word List

about	country	good	may	quick	special	voice
across	cover	great	message	quiet	spell	walk
after	crowd	guess	might	rain	spread	want
again	different	hair	mine	read	spring	was
air	disappear	happy	minute	reason	stand	watch
already	does	heart	money	receive	start	wave
always	down	here	moon	rich	stood	wear
among	drink	high	mother	river	strange	week
animal	drink	horse	mouse	room	strong	whale
area	dry	house	much	round	such	when
around	each	hungry	need	row	sure	which
basket	easy	idea	neighbor	rule	tail	whisper
bear	edge	inch	next	sad	talk	who
because	either	insect	noise	said	taste	why
before	empty	island	nose	same	team	wing
between	enough	join	nothing	save	thank	wire
both	every	just	number	saw	that	with
bought	extra	key	often	school	then	woman
bright	eye	king	once	seat	these	wood
bring	face	kitten	other	seem	thing	work
build	fair	knock	out	several	thought	write
busy	family	know	over	sew	tie	year
came	father	last	page	shoe	tight	young
carry	fence	laugh	paint	shout	today	your
castle	field	lean	park	sick	told	
cause	find	leave	path	sign	took	
children	finger	lesson	pencil	since	toward	
choose	first	life	people	sink	trade	
circle	flake	light	picture	skate	truck	
city	float	listen	plant	sky	turn	
class	floor	long	please	slow	twist	
climb	foot	loud	point	smart	ugly	
cloud	friend	low	poor	snow	under	
coat	full	mail	pretty	some	until	
corner	garden	many	proud	sorry	use	
correct	goes	match	push	south	very	

Words That Work

Read each sentence. Then choose a word from the box to fill in the blank.

dessert	hungry	lesson	whisper	fence	yell
cloud	float	message	castle	guess	desert

1 The teacher wrote the reading _____ on the board.

2 A boat will _____ on water.

3 The smell of baking bread made Andrew _____.

4 The dog jumped over the garden _____.

5 Paul spoke in a low _____.

6 A fluffy _____ moved across the sky.

7 The princess rode toward the stone _____.

8 The _____ was a chocolate chip cake with whipped cream icing.

9 Leah did not know the answer, so she had to _____.

10 Taylor read the _____ from her mother.

11 She had to _____ louder to be heard over the mower.

12 Troy hiked five miles into the hot _____ with his father.

What's in a Word

Look at the word in the first column. In the second column, write a word to describe it. In the third column, write an action word to describe what it can do. The first one is done for you.

	Describing Word	Action Word
1 rabbit	furry	hops
2 car		
3 boat		
4 ball		
5 crayon		
6 snake		
7 drum		
8 butterfly		
9 sun		
10 top		
11 teacher		
12 friend		

Matching Synonyms

Synonyms are words that have the same meaning. For example: *smile* and *grin*.
Match each word in the first column with a word in the second column that has the same meaning.

1 ___ small   a. speedy

2 ___ thin   b. huge

3 ___ cheerful   c. icy

4 ___ decay   d. infant

5 ___ make   e. sob

6 ___ watch   f. shake

7 ___ yell   g. pretty

8 ___ cry   h. giggle

9 ___ beautiful   i. tiny

10 ___ cold   j. create

11 ___ enormous   k. rot

12 ___ tremble   l. slim

13 ___ laugh   m. happy

14 ___ fast   n. shout

15 ___ baby   o. observe

Matching Antonyms

Antonyms are words that have opposite meanings. For example: *dirty* and *clean*.
Match each word in the first column with a word in the second column that has the opposite meaning.

1 ___ top   a. far
2 ___ under   b. sad
3 ___ close   c. awful
4 ___ hot   d. whisper
5 ___ happy   e. bottom
6 ___ asleep   f. nice
7 ___ soft   g. create
8 ___ dull   h. real
9 ___ shout   i. awake
10 ___ float   j. cold
11 ___ wonderful   k. sit
12 ___ mean   l. sharp
13 ___ fake   m. above
14 ___ stand   n. hard
15 ___ destroy   o. sink

Word Wizard

Do you know lots of different words? Show how big your vocabulary is by following the directions below.

1 List four things you would find at the beach:

2 List four words that describe a kitten:

3 List four words that describe your best friend:

4 List four words that describe your favorite teacher:

5 List four words that describe a ride on a roller coaster:

Ready to Rhyme

Rhyming words have the same consonant sounds and ending vowels. For example: *run* and *fun.* Match each word in the first column with a rhyming word in the second column.

1 ___ shake

2 ___ play

3 ___ ring

4 ___ sack

5 ___ wish

6 ___ blew

7 ___ click

8 ___ pot

9 ___ dig

10 ___ moon

11 ___ limp

12 ___ bump

13 ___ crush

14 ___ stuff

15 ___ stand

a. brush

b. brand

c. not

d. lump

e. pig

f. lake

g. sing

h. enough

i. dish

j. back

k. stay

l. new

m. soon

n. shrimp

o. trick

FS122122 The Tutor's Handbook: Reading Grade 3

Find a Rhyme

Now it's time to think of your own rhyming words! Fill in the blanks next to each word with rhyming words. The first one is done for you.

1 cat	sat	bat
2 clock		
3 ball		
4 well		
5 pin		
6 stop		
7 bug		
8 pink		
9 red		
10 bold		
11 stick		
12 chance		
13 stand		
14 brim		
15 tune		

FS122122 The Tutor's Handbook: Reading Grade 3

▷ Name ▷ _____ Date _____

Word Families

A *word family* contains words with the same consonants and ending vowels. For example, *hill, will,* and *still* are all in the same word family. Look at the word endings below. For each one, write three words in the same word family. The first one is done for you.

1 ack	back	rack	lack
2 ake			
3 all			
4 ash			
5 ell			
6 ink			
7 ick			
8 in			
9 ock			
10 op			
11 end			
12 ome			

Building Blends

A blend is a pair or group of letters that makes a special sound. Fill in the missing blends in the sentences below. The first one is done for you.

spr	tr	dr	gr	fl	pl	bl
st	sn	rd	sk	gl	sh	nk	fr

1. The bird flew in the sky.

2. Beautiful ___ owers ___ oom in the ___ ing.

3. The leaves on the ___ ee were ___ een.

4. She read a ___ ory about a ___ agon who likes to ___ ay in the ___ ow.

5. Robin ___ opped her book on the ___ oor.

6. The __ udent ___ ipped open the ___ ue book.

7. Tom ___ ank a ___ ass of ___ ape juice.

8. Marie ___ owed her mother her new pi ___ ___ ess.

9. Jennifer loved ___ owing off magic ___ icks to her ___ iends.

10. Henry climbed the ___ airs up to the ___ uffy, dark attic.

11. That gardening book is about how ___ ails can hurt certain ___ ants.

12. The ___ inklers went off, getting everyone ___ enched.

13. Now make up a sentence of your own using three words with blends.

_____

_____

FS122122 The Tutor's Handbook: Reading Grade 3

Brainstorming Blends

Look at each blend in column one. Write three words after each that contain the
same blend. The blend can be at the beginning, end, or in the middle of the words.
The first one is done for you.

1 st	monster	student	first
2 sn			
3 pr			
4 cr			
5 bl			
6 sk			
7 dr			
8 br			
9 pl			
10 fr			
11 str			
12 tr			

FIRST GRADE PLAY

FS122122 The Tutor's Handbook: Reading Grade 3

Sequencing Sentences

When putting together a paragraph or story, it's important to tell events in the correct order. Otherwise, the reader would be very confused!

Read the following sentences and number them in the correct order.

_____ She opened the door and went outside.
_____ She went to the closet and pulled out her winter coat.
_____ She asked her mother if she could go out and play in the snow.
_____ She began to make a snowman.
_____ Ashley noticed that it was snowing outside.

Read the following paragraph, and then answer the questions below.

Armando went outside to wash his dog, Hamlet. Boy, he was dirty! First, Armando got the tub out of the garage. Then, he got the special dog soap his mom had bought at the pet store—the kind that wouldn't hurt Hamlet's eyes. Next, Armando unwrapped the hose and filled the tub with soap and water. Hamlet sat happily by Armando's side and watched him. But as soon as Armando finished filling the tub, Hamlet ran across the yard and hid behind the bushes!

1 What did Armando do first—go outside, unwrap the hose, or get the

special soap? _____

2 Who bought the special soap? Why?_____

_____

3 When did Hamlet run into the bushes? _____

_____

FS122122 The Tutor's Handbook: Reading Grade 3

Proofing Paragraphs

A *paragraph* is about one main idea. Read each paragraph below and cross out the sentence that does not belong. Then explain why the sentence doesn't make sense in the paragraph.

1 William heard the telephone ring. He went to the kitchen to answer it. It was his friend Marie. She wanted to know if he could go swimming. Marie likes cats. William asked his mother, and she said yes. William rode his bike to Marie's house.

_____

_____

2 The mother bird searched for a worm in the grass. She found a nice plump worm and carried it to her nest. There were three baby birds in the nest. They were all hungry. Worms do not have legs. The mother fed one of her youngsters and then flew away to search for more food.

_____

_____

3 Balloons come in many shapes and sizes. You will often see balloons at birthday parties.Whitney's birthday is on the ninth of June. There are many games you can play with balloons. With practice, you can make animal shapes with them.

_____

_____

The Main Idea

A paragraph must have a *main idea*, or topic. Underline the main idea in each paragraph below.

1 It was a warm day. The sun was shining and there were plenty of people in the park. Hanna and her brother went to the park to play basketball. They brought their lunches with them in brown paper sacks. They started to play, and two other children joined them. At the end of the game, each child had scored two baskets.

2 Mia heard a small cry from behind the garden shed. When she looked to see what had made the noise, she found a tiny kitten. The kitten looked too small to be away from home. Mia thought the little animal was probably hungry. Then she realized this kitten belonged to her neighbor. Mia gently picked up the kitten and took it home.

3 Monday was Lisa's birthday. She invited ten friends to her party. They played games and ate cake. Lisa opened her presents. Among her gifts were two dolls and three stuffed animals. Lisa and her guests had a wonderful time.

4 Jordan was a very talented athlete. He had made the baseball team every year so far, and he was voted most valuable player at last year's banquet. He had even broken two of the school's long-standing records. He was sure to get a scholarship to college!

Who? What? Where? When?

When retelling a story, you should be able to tell *who, what, where,* and *when.*
These are the important parts of a story. They answer the questions:

- *Who is the story about?*
- *What happened?*
- *Where did it happen?*
- *When did it happen?*

Write *who, what, where,* or *when* to
describe each phrase below.

AND THEN SHE LOOKED UNDER THE BED...

1 _____ under the bed

2 _____ her sister

3 _____ after the party

4 _____ it rained hard

5 _____ over the fence

6 _____ ate the salad

7 _____ jumped the rope

8 _____ behind the chair

9 _____ Aunt Laura

10 _____ the farmer

11 _____ ten brown rabbits

12 _____ at 5:00 p.m.

13 _____ just in time

14 _____ laughed out loud

15 _____ all the cousins

16 _____ ran for cover

17 _____ in the shed

18 _____ gathered tomatoes

19 _____ between the houses

20 _____ Kylie and Ryan

FS122122 The Tutor's Handbook: Reading Grade 3

Name _____ Date _____

My Book Review

Title of Book: _____

Author: _____

This book was (hard/easy) because _____

_____

_____

I enjoyed/did not enjoy this book because _____

_____

_____

When I listened to the story, I thought _____

_____

_____

When I read the story, I thought _____

_____

_____

I would/would not read this story again because _____

_____

_____

On the back of this page, list some things you learned by

reading this book.

I Predict . . .

Before Reading

Title of Book: _____

Author: _____

I think this book will be about: _____

_____

I think the main character is: _____

This is how I think the book will end: _____

_____

_____

****

After Reading

The book was about: _____

_____

_____

The main character was: _____

This is how the story ended: _____

_____

_____

 **Name** _____ Date _____

READING AWARD

This special Reading Award is presented to

_____

for learning how to use good reading strategies.

Congratulations! You are learning to be a terrific reader—
a whole new world of adventure awaits you!

_____   _____

(Tutor)   (Student)

FS122122 The Tutor's Handbook: Reading Grade 3

Answer Key

Words That Work (page 47)
1. lesson
2. float
3. hungry
4. fence
5. whisper
6. cloud
7. castle
8. dessert
9. guess
10. message
11. yell
12. desert

What's in a Word (page 48)
Answers will vary.

Matching Synonyms (page 49)
1. small/tiny
2. thin/slim
3. cheerful/happy
4. decay/rot
5. make/create
6. watch/observe
7. yell/shout
8. cry/sob
9. beautiful/pretty
10. cold/icy
11. enormous/huge
12. tremble/shake
13. laugh/giggle
14. fast/speedy
15. baby/infant

Matching Antonyms (page 50)
1. top/bottom
2. under/above
3. close/far
4. hot/cold
5. happy/sad
6. asleep/awake
7. soft/hard
8. dull/sharp
9. shout/whisper
10. float/sink
11. wonderful/awful
12. mean/nice
13. fake/real
14. stand/sit
15. destroy/create

Word Wizard (page 51)
Answers will vary.

Ready to Rhyme (page 52)
1. shake/lake
2. play/stay
3. ring/sing
4. sack/back
5. wish/dish
6. blew/new
7. click/trick
8. pot/not
9. dig/pig
10. moon/soon
11. limp/shrimp
12. bump/lump
13. crush/brush
14. stuff/enough
15. stand/brand

Find a Rhyme (page 53)
Answers will vary.

Word Families (page 54)
Answers will vary.

Building Blends (page 55)
1. The bird flew in the sky.
2. Beautiful flowers bloom in the spring.
3. The leaves on the tree were green.
4. She read a story about a dragon who likes to play in the snow.
5. Robin dropped her book on the floor.
6. The student flipped open the blue book.
7. Tom drank a glass of grape juice.
8. Marie showed her mother her new pink dress.
9. Jennifer loved showing off magic tricks to her friends.
10. Henry climbed the stairs up to the stuffy, dark attic.
11. That gardening book is about how snails can hurt certain plants.
12. The sprinklers went off, getting everyone drenched.
13. Answers will vary.

Brainstorming Blends (page 56)
Answers will vary.

Sequencing Sentences (page 57)
Correct sentence sequence:
1 –Ashley noticed that it was snowing outside.
2 –She asked her mother if she could go out and play in the snow.
3 –She went to the closet and pulled out her winter coat.
4 –She opened the door and went outside.
5 –She began to make a snowman.

1. Armando went outside.
2. His mother; because it wouldn't hurt Hamlet's eyes.
3. Hamlet ran into the bushes as soon as Armando finished filling the tub.

Proofing Paragraphs (page 58)
1. Cross out: *Marie likes cats.* The paragraph is about William and Marie going swimming, not cats.
2. Cross out: *Worms do not have legs.* The paragraph is about a mother bird feeding her young, not about worms.
3. Cross out: *Whitney's birthday is on the ninth of June.* The paragraph is about balloons; not Whitney's birthday.
   Explanations will vary.

The Main Idea (page 59)
1. Hanna and her brother went to the park to play basketball.
2. Mia found a tiny kitten.
3. Monday was Lisa's birthday.
4. Jordan was a very talented athlete.

Who? What? Where? When? (page 60)
1. where
2. who
3. when
4. what
5. where
6. what
7. what
8. where
9. who
10. who
11. who or what
12. when
13. when
14. what
15. who
16. what
17. where
18. what
19. where
20. who